Ode to a
Very Stable Genius

Ode to a
Very Stable Genius
A QUATRAIN COMPENDIUM WITH PICTURES

Carl Powlett

ILLUSTRATIONS
Jordan Couttien

POWLETT ENTERPRISES
Brooklyn NY 11233
powlettenterprises.com

Illustrations by Jordan Couttien

First Edition: August 2020

Library of Congress Control Number: 2020914164

ISBN 978-0-578-73714-0 (Paperback)
ISBN 978-0-578-74349-3   (eBook)

for **Colin Powlett**

Remember.
Always tell the truth.
Even when it appears you may be disadvantaged.

for **Christopher Van Bell**

Thank you.
This collaboration would not have
been possible without your heroic act.

A storyteller makes up things to help other people;
a liar makes up things to help himself.

-- Daniel Wallace, *Writer*

Still, when I think of the road we're traveling on
I wonder what went wrong.
I can't help it, I wonder what went wrong.

-- Paul Simon, *"American Tune"*

Not enjoyment, and not sorrow,
Is our destined end or way;
But to act, that each tomorrow
Finds us farther than today.

-- Henry Wadsworth Longfellow, *"A Psalm of Life"*

When you see something that is not right,
you must say something. You must do something.

-- John Lewis, *American Hero*

Preface

Where did this come from? I think it was the hand of God, but, possibly, Satan's. I hope it was the former, but given the subject of the verses in this book, the latter cannot be ruled out.

Late one night, several weeks ago, after reading a *New York Times* op-ed by Frank Bruni about Donald Trump's missing soul, I was scrolling through the accompanying reader comments when a poetic verse erupted in my mind. Immediately, I switched to my Notes App and wrote the verse. Within a few minutes, I had tapped out a stanza.

The rhythm was reminiscent to that of a poem I had written in 2012, titled, *"Thank You, Mr. Romney,"* in celebration of Justice Roberts giving the Supreme Court's stamp of approval to Obamacare. Then I wrote a second stanza. Then a third. I was unable to sleep. By the time I fell asleep, several hours later, I had completed eight stanzas.

Within a few days, I had drummed out forty-four stanzas. I willed myself to complete another, thinking that, given the subject, forty-five was an appropriate number. Yet, I persisted. Either divinely, or demonically driven.

Donald Trump was the gift that kept on giving. His every utterance – past, present, and, it would turn out, future – became fodder for an ever-expanding composition I chose to name, *"Ode to a Very Stable Genius."*

Carl V. Powlett
Brooklyn, New York
April 25, 2020

Introduction

If I were Donald Trump, I would tell you that the poem you are about to read contains more than five hundred perfectly executed quatrains. Moreover, many people are saying there may be over one thousand.

Both assertions would be easily verifiable lies.

Donald Trump doesn't just lie; he *is* a liar.

Of course, Donald J. Trump requires no introduction. We must live with the knowledge of who he is and what that means for our daily lives and future. The time has long passed since I exhausted my lexicon on "Reader Comments" to a variety of publications, excoriating "Putin's Puppet."

There were no descriptives left. The words were different, but the sentiment repetitive. Even though Trump had lost the popular vote, there were still tens of millions of my fellow citizens who unconditionally adored their President. I read the explanations, listened to the punditry, tried to unravel the tortured rationales. I continue to be confounded, overwhelmed, dismayed.

Donald John Trump is a willfully ignorant, dangerously uninformed, contemptible, braggart of a man. He is and should continue to be the poster child for white privilege. Its Epitome. The man who managed to ride failure after failure to the top. Remarkable! Presto! The Winner!

I never intended or planned to write about the self-proclaimed "Very Stable Genius." The first verse of the now unremembered initial stanza sprang from me late one night. As more verses and stanzas materialized, I observed, unbidden, they had coalesced into quatrains filled with sardonic expressions of admiration for "The Donald's" all-embracing perfection, written from the perspective of his rabid supporters. I deliberately decided to continue in this manner. After writing the forty-fifth, which was to have been my final stanza, and, incidentally, remains as such in this compendium, I stopped.

However, soon thereafter, I came awake in the middle of the night, reached for a pencil and sticky note, and sleepily scrawled: *Because it's you our SG this ode had to be gigantic no simple haiku couplet could suffice for a legend so fantastic*, and I went back to sleep.

When I greeted the new day, it was clear to me I would continue writing. At the same time, I felt I needed to begin the poem with something contextual. A stanza or two that would set the tone for what would follow. As it was, a path had opened a few hours earlier when I had drunkenly scribbled that grammatically challenged run-on.

Until then, I had been writing for my enjoyment. Now, a desire to publish the work took hold of me. Surely, with this burst of creativity, I could achieve one hundred stanzas.

I checked a 1963 edition of a book of poems from my schoolboy days for the longest poem I'd read, *"The Rime of the Ancient Mariner,"* by Samuel Taylor Coleridge. There are about one hundred and forty-five stanzas of *primarily* ABCB quatrains. I vowed to write one hundred and fifty and committed to the already established ABCB rhyme scheme of my effort, I elected to write without any punctuation. I'd leave it to the reader to decide on the rhythm and cadence of each verse.

Having heard or read Donald Trump described as a "narcissist" countless times, I resolved not to use that word. Further, to not use his name until the final stanza, which, as previously noted, had already been written.

I wanted a prologue and epilogue but knew I would not attempt a narrative chronology. Such a thing would require many, many months of full-time focus. Fortunately, the stanzas I had already written could each stand-alone (In the final work, there are a few instances where two or more related stanzas follow consecutively). Thus, the compendium.

Astonishingly, that same morning, I wrote the initial six stanzas of the prologue in about fifteen minutes, using the nocturnal jotting as a starting point. This middle-of-the-night scribbling was reset (I had scribbled it in the past tense, ostensibly making it more suitable for the epilogue), and became the first quatrain.

The others[1] just flowed out. Several weeks later, I added a seventh, after my wife shared a meme of Trump and his mother.

As I continued to write past the first hundred stanzas, inspired by, and, from reader comments from various publications, and Trump's daily meanderings, I thought of the potential for repetition. However, there is a great deal to be said about my subject; the swill runs wide. If anything, having exceeded Coleridge's seven-score-plus count, and my target of one hundred and fifty, the larger concern became my apparent inability to bring the project to a close.

Each day brought new and different topics, in addition to discoveries of past controversies, disputes, affairs, and goings-on I had missed. And then, for a day or so, I fixated on the disgraceful, black-hearted, diabolical William Barr.

Trump could not be the tyrant he is, if Barr, or someone like him, did not exist. The AG's name would turn out to be the one most documented in this publication.

In my mind's eye, I saw the two as puppet and puppeteer. But who was which? I wasn't sure. That dyslexic-like moment embedded a mental image that I aspired to manifest. My granddaughter, Jordan, is a very talented artist. With some guidance, she produced the illustration of Trump and Barr, or, maybe, Barr and Trump, which became the image for the book cover. She signed on to produce a few more.

Heaven knows, there's no shortage of books about our accidental President. I suspect, however, there is no other four-hundred-plus stanza poem, with original sketches to boot.

We are a nation that has come to prize entertainment over education. As such, I attempted to inject as much humor as seemed appropriate, for a

---

[1]The 2nd stanza of the poem's "Prologue" includes the phrase **"between time and Timbuktu."** For many readers, this may require clarification: In the mid-seventies, I, and a co-worker, Neville McKen, discovered the works of Kurt Vonnegut. *"Between Time and Timbuktu or Prometheus-5,"* was a title whose meaning we puzzled over. After much discussion over a period of days, having consulted a dictionary, Neville said he believed Vonnegut was referring to everything in the universe, which was represented by all the words in the dictionary, reading forward from "time" and then coming back around to "Timbuktu," immediately preceding "time." I found no fault with that assessment. Thus, an "exhaustive" composition would require that **everything** related to a subject is included, i.e., the spaces between time and Timbuktu.

subject which, at its core, can seem quite grim. Sarcasm can and does cut both ways. There's a lot of cutting here.

America has been and continues to be a great nation. To say otherwise is disingenuous. It is a great nation with an (over?)-abundance of shortcomings, but one that remains a work in progress.

The electoral elevation of Donald Trump brought many deeply-rooted, longstanding, demonstrable, yet still, globally unacknowledged, unsettled, unsettling inequities and disparities into the unobstructed daylight of the public square, both physical and virtual. Much of it, rooted in America's "original sin," slavery. Racism. Further, and, arguably, equally as important, we stumbled upon the realization that the democratic structures upon which we depend, are not as reliable as we thought.

One man (with a little help from his friends), if so disposed, can substantively degrade, if not destroy, the values and ideals of the nation. No, it is not a perfect union. It never was. Still, even during past periods of strident civil disagreements and discord, we, the people, as a fractured collective, appeared to have understood that the goal has always been to steer toward a more perfect union.

Donald Trump could not care less.

Cynically, he's been encouraged and enabled by a political cadre and legions of cultist worshippers. Their distorted ideals and values are uninhibited by age-old virtues of respect, fairness, acceptance, compassion, kindness, equality, justice, and duty. Nevertheless, these are virtues they hypocritically claim to embrace.

Under Trump, racist dog whistles, which Republicans have consistently employed, with varying degrees of success since Lyndon Johnson's Great Society programs, have become full-blown, unavoidable foghorns. The in-your-face, unashamed, unapologetic use of the Southern Strategy, fashioned for the Twitterverse.

It's all about trying to ensure their party remains in control, even when out of power. Forget about what is fair or what is right. To hell with what is good for the health and maintenance of a vibrant democratic republic.

It's late July, as I write this. The United States of America remains a democracy. More tenuous than it's ever been. Yet, still functioning within the constraints of its founding principles.

Thomas Jefferson said the people are the only sure reliance for the preservation of liberty. In spite of 2016, the ballot is still the best change agent we have.

With the recent death of Congressman John Lewis, we are reminded of the monumental sacrifices untold numbers of other heroic men and women, especially, Black people, have made, in order to get and keep that franchise – the essence of our representative democracy. Voting, i.e., the right to freely and easily vote, is foundational.

In this age of Trump and sustained, coordinated, multi-pronged attacks from embedded establishment voting rights revanchists, wielding the ballot has never been more important for the well-being of this always struggling democracy.

Siri just informed me that November 3rd is ninety-nine days hence. No doubt, Trump will increase the chaos upon which he seems to thrive, in the hope that his supporters will inundate the polls and his detractors will stay away. He has become more vociferous in his campaign to discredit the tried and true method of voting by mail, with continuing attempts to cripple the U.S. Postal Service through surrogate "Acting" stooges and other sycophants.

Almost five decades ago, when Gerald Ford replaced the last President who brought us to the brink of a constitutional crisis, he said that our national nightmare was over. Let's pray that on the night of November 3, 2020, we can, with a high degree of certainty, declare the same.

These quatrains touch upon practically every aspect of the life and times of this perfidious, hollow man – past, present, hoped for, and imagined. An ode is meant to be a poem of adoration, worship, adulation – a paean.

Certainly, this one has a boatload of the kind of superlatives that should leave our famously swellheaded POTUS with a permanent Mona Lisa smile. However, the denouement of a plurality of stanzas, invariably belie the approbation of the "A" verse; they are poetic chameleons. If these should be read to him (One gets the feeling he may have avoided the remedial ELA at Wharton), his reaction is likely to be more Munch than Leonardo.

With this literary effort, my hope is, readers will find lines, phrases, segments (Alas, not everyone is a gem), that will lead to further exploration, knowledge, and understanding. Maybe, even, clarity. It's the kind of book a reader (non-regular readers, too) can pick up at any time. It could be a fine substitute for the TV remote. It doesn't need batteries and isn't likely to get lost between the seat cushions.

Appreciating most of the verses require only a passing knowledge of current events. There are a few esoteric entries for news junkies and worse (or, better) - historians. Also, some which may, not unreasonably, be labeled as "puzzling" (à la the one that includes the spices, parsley, sage, rosemary, and thyme).

I have taken a leap of faith, that readers of this book are a curious bunch (Loads of bunches?), who will take the time to consider the possible "puzzlement" (Privy Pantheon?) within the context of the verse, stanza, and its relationship to the subject. So.

Read.

Enjoy.

Stay safe. Socially distance.

Wear a mask. Believe in Science.

Vote. It matters.

Tell the truth. Always.

PROLOGUE

Prologue

Because it's you our Stable Genius
This Ode has to be fantastic
No simple haiku or couplet will do
For an ego so gigantic

We don't know if we can be exhaustive
There's so much to be said about you
But we'll work hard to fill in the spaces
That are between time and Timbuktu

Fifth Avenue was the scene of the crime
The victim lay dead on the ground
You held the smoking gun in your hand
The cop looked at you and turned around

Like a horse led to the water's edge
A Wharton education's meant to nourish
Just as the equine can't be made to drink
Some minds go to school yet still perish

Heaven knows you are never wrong
Why hold conflicting views in your mind
No need to know what you don't know
You're a Very Stable Genius in your prime

There's no denying our Stable Genius
You said you take no responsibility
Folks may not realize that's not new
It's the centerpiece of your life strategy

There's a meme out there with Mom and you
It claims she said you're an idiot
You'd be a disaster in politics she submits
It's amazing you dodged being inadequate

1

JORDAN COUTIEN

Ode to a
Very Stable Genius

I

You know we love sarcasm Stable Genius
Though whenever we try we come up short
You are the masterful practitioner
For you the deed seems like an afterthought

You are our savior Stable Genius
We are certain it was not Barack
Two thousand years is a long time to wait
No way would HE be a Negro Democrat

We want much more of you our Stable Genius
Eight years won't be nearly enough
The 2nd Amendment is our friend
We could make you an American caliph

There's no other like you Stable Genius
You told us you're the best
You met the moment and prevailed
Your singularity is manifest

When you invented prime the pump
The world was agape at your sagacity
Two decades after Dunning-Kruger
Some say you confirmed their theory

An African American in Charleston EssCee
Said we're blessed that you enlightened us
We would never have known its significance
If you had not made Juneteenth very famous

II

Your talent is limitless Stable Genius
You're better than Edgar Bergen
Your ventriloquism is undeniably displayed
Whenever Bill Barr's mouth opens

We sing your praises our Stable Genius
For your unprecedented electoral victory
Despite three million fraudulent ballots
You changed the course of history

How did we ever live without you
With men like George Abe and Barack
These guys were clearly lightweights
In you we found our crackerjack

Your crowd was the largest since antiquity
Down from the Capitol and out to the sea
Just like with Woodstock people have said
An historic turnout and precipitation free

What do we have to lose you asked
Why not take a chance on you
Others have failed us again and again
What are the odds that you would too

As a nation we are beholden to you
You privilege the present over the future
You agitate fabricate and fulminate
You leave us filled with wonder

III

You promise total freedom
It's the way you've led your life
Taken what you wanted when you wanted
You are the man to set us right

We'd like to thank you Stable Genius
You're omniscient in all things
No need for bumbling experts
By George you are The King

Some hag said you can't be royalty
That your Barron can't be a baron
At least you've earned a sunlit throne
A seat of honor in the Privy Pantheon

God bless YOUR Attorney General
He's Apostle Paul to you our Savior
You anointed him to deliver
Truly he's your greatest protector

We love that you activated Bill Barr
We love that you activated him strongly
He's a man who knows how to DOMINATE
He's not physically weak nor personally cowardly

You're the leader we always pined for
Though we didn't know it at the start
Now we welcome you with alacrity
Our warm and cuddly Bonaparte

IV

Like a meteorologist par excellence
The Predictor of the true course of storms
When weathervanes and satellites fail
You Stable Genius will not misinform

You have done so much for religion
The Book of Me should be your gospel
With your Sermons from the Bunker
Surely your name will be immortal

We'd like to thank you Stable Genius
Your piety is beautiful to behold
Evangelicals extol your virtues
Knowing your coming was foretold

The greatest liar has his believers
Thank God that does not apply to us
You are a right and truthful messenger
A bible and you together are priceless

You love the Lord our Stable Genius
But you've never taken to your knees
We're happy to see you won't give solace
To Colin Kaepernick and his coterie

It's OK not to know The Star-Spangled Banner
There are too many words and it's not melodic
We've seen solid proof of your devotion
Hugging and kissing the flag is truly patriotic

V

We'd like to thank you Stable Genius
For your moral compass straight and true
No doubt our kids feel obligated
To follow the example set by you

You made it cool to lie and bully
To swear and mock and jeer
Who needs permission to grab crotches
You set the guilt-free atmosphere

We'd like to thank you Stable Genius
For teaching us romance
We now know stormy dalliances
Can be calmed by high finance

We're tickled pink with your transparency
You tell us what you're thinking
You say the quiet parts out loud
Yet so much remains confusing

You are committed our Stable Genius
We can always count on you
First you'll say no then you'll say yes
And the inverse is also true

This is self-evident Stable Genius
There's no one wiser in this millennium
No need to go searching for metrics
They're domiciled in the cavity of your cranium

VERY STABLE GENIUS

JORDAN COUTTEN

VI

Now and again we wonder
Why you've never shared your GPA
Undoubtedly it is phenomenal
A source of pride and privilege

We are in awe our Stable Genius
You have a gift for contradictions
The irony does not escape us
You build the Wall and raze the Constitution

We revere you Stable Genius
Your name is prominent in many fields
Travel Gaming Education Philanthropy
Ill-fated examples of the art of the deal

We adore you Stable Genius
For that beautiful Mexican wall
Doesn't matter they didn't pay for it
It doesn't matter at all

You're our beacon Stable Genius
Our Shining City on the Hill
Both an example and a warning
An idyll with cancer causing windmills

Some say we're losing our old Exceptionalism
There's just a rotting vestige of that trait
Xenophobia greed dishonesty incompetence
The new exceptional things we now embrace

VII

Thank you for great new friendships
That NATO thing is so passé
We need strongman connections
Democracy's so yesterday

You might remember our Stable Genius
We fought to liberate Europe
Now they say we can't come over
What did we do to mess things up

You are the avatar of America First
Shunning alliances and multilateralism
No need for the UN or the G7
Organizations brimming with elitism

We love that you're our own Dear Leader
Our Vlad Our Kim Our Xi
Shirtless and bold on a trusty steed
A fighter for old greatness and autocracy

You shouldn't have to push to the front row
These other leaders should step aside
You own any room you're in Stable Genius
They should act in a manner more dignified

How dare Angela refuse your invitation
Maggie would never have done that to Ron
Go ahead and pull our troops out of Deutschland
Teach her what it feels like to be spurned

VIII

We worship you our Stable Genius
Our twenty-first century Gipper
Where Ronnie was good for only a trickle
You managed to bring home a gusher

You are our fiddler on the roof
Battling the besiegers of our traditions
With you we know our country's safe
You are the master of fortifications

Environmentally you stand tall and proud
A voice in the wilderness not part of the crowd
Climate's in danger reckless scientists scream
But you Stable Genius are a redwood unbowed

That Greta Thunberg's such an airhead
Small carbon footprint tiny brain
Who takes a boat cross the Atlantic
When there are so many beautiful planes

We applaud you Stable Genius
For rolling back Obama's regulations
He cared too little about the present
Far too much for future generations

You made America great again
With your fifteen-to-zero plan
The nation gasped in disbelief
As we shot up to number one

IX

We'd like to thank you Stable Genius
For helping us forget
The burden that democracy is
We are forever in your debt

Some Conservatives say you're a liar
They're losers who can't get on FOX
A rabid willfully ignorant minority
Who believe Lincoln lived in the projects

There's no need for us to speak up
We far outnumber losers who take to the streets
The silent majority is on your side
Though it would be nice to have your niece

Those beautiful Confederate monuments are ours
We ought to fight for their preservation
There were very fine people on both sides
Why fuss over a misguided secession

We'll always be with you Stable Genius
No need to try hard to keep us engaged
We don't really care who the other guy is
As long as it's you we'll be outraged

A future without you our Stable Genius
Would unleash a wave of violent crime
The others think us weak soft and submissive
There'll be shock and awe when we shift that paradigm

X

It's the economy stupid Clinton contended
One of the few things he said that was true
In the midst of a crippling pandemic
That admonition is not lost on you

Speaking of William Jefferson
There may be a dress with your DNA
That writer from Bergdorf never had it cleaned
It seems for her it was a memorable day

You're legendary Stable Genius
Your conquests are considerable
Decades on many still ask
If you'll ever be held accountable

Some say you're like the Pied Piper
Others say you're more like Pinocchio
Though we like Very Stable Genius best
We are also partial to Nero

Our media is the enemy of the people
No wonder some got Noble Prizes
We're guessing those are like Pulitzers
Only given to the worse writers

We'd like to thank you Stable Genius
For speaking English so sublime
Our children are encouraged
To know they too can make the climb

XI

Clearly you've earned a face on Rushmore
You've changed the nation like no other
A thousand years from now people should know
Though ravaged by a plague we kept our sense of humor

You are Churchillian our Stable Genius
You know how to summon us to action
There's no one better to stir up the nation
Your words can evoke deep emotions

Thank you Stable Genius
We now know the cost of ignorance
Without you steering the ship of state
We may never have found our tolerance

We approve of you Stable Genius
You know how to own the Libs
Soaring boasts and searing grievances
And beautiful incredible fibs

Go back to the countries they came from
You're right to have put them in their place
When each was elected to Congress
She should have ceased parading in blackface

You pulled yourself up by your bootstraps
After Daddy's gazillions were gone
Your heel spurs no longer a bother
Those Deutsche brogues eased right on

JORDAN COUTTIEN

XII

We thank you Stable Genius
For all the debt that you bestowed
It's our children's bedtime favorite
A tale whose end remains untold

Like casinos that fail in boom times
We'd puzzled at how that could be
But thanks to you Stable Genius
That's no longer a mystery

We'd like to thank you Stable Genius
You made us what we are today
We cherish our newfound isolation
That trillion-dollar deficit's OK

Being President has cost you billions
We feel your financial pain
However we do take some comfort
That your golf games are a gravy train

The Fed could not reserve without you
At counseling their governors you excel
You're a monument in monetary policy
A Taj Mahal too big to fail

You are the ultimate CEO
You know how to discipline the working class
Messages full of content devoid of meaning
And the illusion they're not second class

XIII

It's a puzzlement we relish our Stable Genius
The oxymoron called the Black supporter
We think it's a metaphor for all Americans
Your mysterious appeal is most peculiar

It's disgraceful how bad Obama was
Each day of your term he gets worse
We fear Stable Genius if you have four more years
He may put all you've done in reverse

To you Power transcends democracy
Debate impedes expediency
Only you can fix what ails us
You must be the sole authority

You are our LAW & ORDER President
We must ensure your survival
You must insist on going to your bunker
When vociferous protestors come over

The rule of law is yours to make
We venerate your judicious mind
You command judges and Justices too
You Stable Genius know justice isn't blind

God put you in charge for the moment
To bring back Christmas and Greatness
To bar restrictions on liberty
Exalt Christianity and homogeneity

XIV

Tu es l'état our Stable Genius
Louis XIV would envy you
It's sad you won't rule as long as he did
Though Hydroxy may come to the rescue

We weren't pleased with the VP in this instance
Why didn't he take Hydroxy
He claimed his doctor hadn't recommended it
Contrary to your guiding philosophy

You're our indispensable national treasure
Fit for a lifetime presidency
With a genius like you it's time for adieu
To the limit on White House occupancy

I'd rather be a Russian than a Democrat
A sentiment we can't help but share
There'd be zero pride being an American
If ever we looked up and you weren't there

The 2nd Amendment does not bar the misguided
Reverential men armed with AR-15s
If you're not the victor will they go to war
Elections are anathema to aspiring sovereigns

You get it Stable Genius
The forty-four before were beginners
Those who voted and lost are not your concern
Your job is to care for the winners

XV

We idolize you Stable Genius
Success begets success they say is true
Susan Collins said you'd learned your lesson
She must have misremembered it was you

We rejoice in the unshackling of impeachment
It's the ideal time for reckoning
Inspectors General and prosecutors will feel the sting
Their meddling and interference can bring

Quid pro quo quid pro quo
All that sound and fury
When you negotiated in the past
Contractors knew there'd be injury

You make or break political careers
Sessions must get his comeuppance
His recusal was a disloyal betrayal
Squeeze him till he loses his political pulse

You're a big tall man our Stable Genius
Just a tad below Abe Lincoln
You are both monumental in many ways
Though you always fall short by a smidgen

What's ours is yours Stable Genius
We agree it was meant to be
E Pluribus Unum actually means
Belonging to the bourgeoisie

XVI

You taught us all about humility
Honesty loyalty duty and trust
We've come to marvel at their absence
Who needs these values in a putsch

Thank you for your unrepentance
We're tired of spineless leadership
Emoluments should be a perk of the job
Who better than you to flaunt it

One hundred and thirty-eight million
That's what we paid for your golfing so far
We think it's a pittance our Stable Genius
You could have made billions as a TV star

We are devoted to you our Stable Genius
We affirm your conspicuous magnificence
You are MacGyver to our broken nation
Fully equipped with inborn contrivance

Can't praise you enough Stable Genius
Platitudes never get old with you
You're Gibraltar Everest Fuji too
Lowbrow adjectives would never do

We trust you implicitly our Stable Genius
Like the George who never told a lie
He ran Mount Vernon from the Oval Office
With two desks standing side by side

XVII

We are awestruck Stable Genius
You're a whisperer of viruses and plagues
When April arrives the doubters we know
Will choke on their clueless mistakes

You're our rock star Stable Genius
You play the soundtrack of our lives
We're tuned to Make America Great Again
The timeless classic Live Free or Die

Democrats hate our history and values
Everything we prize as Americans
The left-wing mob will destroy our heritage
That's why God made you OUR Republican

Storm the legislature with no masks on
Armed with their AR-15s
Our Boogaloos are ready to die for FREEDOM
To hell with Whitmer's quarantine

We know that masks aren't about health
They are about submission
The mandate came from the Deep State
Just one more step towards our subjugation

They cannot escape God with their devil's laws
Telling patriots to wear masks that block oxygen
We will follow your lead our Stable Genius
Should it kill us we're going to heaven

XVIII

Through bankruptcies divorces many scandals
You've proved you are a survivor
We're sticking with you our Stable Genius
You've mastered the mediocre

Daily briefings are worthless
To a man whose knowledge is limitless
You're the fountainhead of enlightenment
The exemplification of genius

You're The Greatest Stable Genius
Muhammad Ali stands below you
You'd never rumble in a jungle
Places only good for number twos

We are blessed to bask in your entitlement
As you shun darkness and admit the light
We see again our Stable Genius
Now orange is the new White

Your compassion is so transparent
It's like the king's new clothes
Regardless of how you try to hide it
Your true nature remains exposed

You're hard-boiled our Stable Genius
Out damn spot is your command to a dog
Lady Macbeth was weak in a big way
A guilty conscience belongs in a synagogue

XIX

You don't do empathy our Stable Genius
That seems completely natural
Why try to be the man you're not
That would be irrational

It's not innate for you our Stable Genius
Articulating condolence requires a script
Nevertheless the performance always sputters
Even when well-prepared you're ill-equipped

You have no reason to treat Scarborough fair
There was a relationship with Thyme
Though Sage said he was with Rosemary
Parsley saw him at the scene of the crime

Birtherism was hard to pin down
Here's something else to ply
Isn't it strange that he was born
The day Marilyn Monroe died

That Buffalo grandpa is a very fine actor
Trained at the Antifa School for Ancient Thespians
A small push became a giant fall for the cause
Blood dripping from his ear enriched his performance

A platform built for threats and ridicule
Custom-made for a genius like you
Should not be modified in any way
Why do tweets have to be true

XX

Your native intelligence is peerless
There's nothing analysts can teach you
While other Presidents required briefings
You have your Gut to guide you

Most doctors are amazed at what you know
Thanks to your natural ability and Uncle MIT
Though some have mentioned maladministration
Abysmal leadership and mendacity

This doesn't happen often Stable Genius
But we think we have a great idea
You should spend a day as a substitute teacher
The missus can help you prepare

We'd like to thank you Stable Genius
For gelding our silly Congress
Your exceptional Constitutional acumen
Has rendered them virtually useless

We glory in your good fortune
McConnell Graham Kushner Giuliani
Loyal men of singular vision
Each as steadfast as Robert E Lee

You are the Voice of America
Your words paint an inimitable image
We don't need propaganda radio
Competing with your eloquent message

XXI

You're always right our Stable Genius
Everyone else is wrong
You've earned universal obsequiousness
And this Little Red Book like Mao Zedong

Because we lack your erudition Stable Genius
We were unaware that we are Paleocons
Some donkey said we also are Revanchists
Why have we never seen these words on FOX chyrons

We are truly blessed you're our greatest builder
Other lesser ethnic builders tell us so
With generations of immigrant builders in their lineage
Who better than they to know

You are the cleverest our Stable Genius
Though your syntax is not confirmative
We think that you deliberately stumble
To further numb the ovine masses

Just as with all things under the sun
You know more than the generals
We take for granted you won every skirmish
And shrapnel never pierced your femoral

Your grasp of military doctrine is elemental
It is a gift from a mystical power
You denounce the injustice of war crime convictions
By picturing yourself in the boots of the soldier

JORDAN COUTTIEN

XXII

When in your great and unmatched wisdom
You pulled our troops out of Syria
Tayyip and Vlad were said to have smiled
In homage to the stratagem of a true master

You made the Greatest Economy in History
Which was brought down by The Invisible Enemy
But being much larger than the moment
You'll bring an even greater recovery

You're incredible Stable Genius
You say incredible genius things
That's why we don't think it's incredible
You're incredibly loved by lemmings

If not for your innate perfection
So much could be blamed on you
But why should you take responsibility
When no one else seems to have a clue

We exalt you Stable Genius
You should govern every state
Imagine how great you *would* work with you
There would be no need for debate

Much like you our Stable Genius
Hydroxychloroquine is God's gift we must try
Those who say you're being cavalier
Have evidently never died

XXIII

We know Stable Genius you pretend
That Intelligence isn't your bailiwick
When you seem to ignore sage advice
You are simply being Socratic

Unemployment is a totally phony number
You said that when Obama's were good
Your opinion seems to have become fact
Unless your number has been misunderstood

Pay down debt in a boom is the rule
Take on debt in a recession
You're the great contrarian Stable Genius
Freud should have treated Keynes for depression

Resentful others yelp that you are privileged
Unlike yours their color is hard to reside in
You were handed the riches of Croesus
How sad that you wasted your white skin

We hear it all the time that you are stupid
Kind of like saying that sunshine is opaque
They're just green with envy Stable Genius
You can't be stupid if you never make mistakes

There may come a day our Stable Genius
When our party reunites with its conscience
Until that day with you we'll make hay
Thumbing our nose at emoluments

XXIV

From your lips to Our Father's ears
We know that Mueller lied
His just reward is at the Pearly Gates
Yours we think is on the hotter side

Thank you for that fallow Senate
It needed time to rest
We hope when Moscow Mitch awakens
There'll be more Dems to dispossess

The Senate is the graveyard of legislation
They say the stench marks the decay of Congress
That chamber's done exactly what you wanted
Very Stable Genius our own Caesar Augustus

You're a hero to birthers everywhere
From an acorn to a great oak you grew it
Persuading the historically challenged
That Hawaii is not a legitimate state

You have little to lose our Stable Genius
Covid-19 doesn't dwell well with MAGA
Your base need not fear the coronavirus
It seems partial to La Casa de Shaka

All Black lives matter
Not just their gangstas
Tyson Kanye that boxing promoter
And let's not forget Robin Quivers

XXV

Your Younger Genius called BLM animals
Reminiscent of you and the Central Park Five
We're gratified the apple didn't fall far from the tree
Your insights and wisdom must be kept alive

You're our rock Stable Genius
Deeply rooted impossible to bend
The Central Park Five your bête noire cinq
Is one conviction you'd never rescind

13.3% unemployment is mission accomplished
You think George Floyd would have been proud
But the note in the report states it's a mistake
Good thing he didn't have to stick his neck out

The concept of chokeholds sounds so innocent so perfect
Reminiscent of your Zelensky phone call
Some say in practice it is depraved and abhorrent
Much like your Zelensky phone call

Obamacare is such a mess
The worse thing ever done by Congress
Except of course the Iranian deal
NAFTA and yes Freedom of the Press

We aren't as visionary as you our Stable Genius
We acknowledge you have our best interests at heart
Still it confounds us in our quiet moments
Why you're so eager to tear the ACA apart

XXVI

We heard The Blacks aren't doing well
That's not really news
Question is will they now vote for you
Certainly they have nothing to lose

It's not a close call our Stable Genius
You've done so much more for The Blacks
Sure Lincoln did the Emancipation
But you didn't propose a new poll tax

Scum Scum human Scum FBI conspiracy
We feel the depth of your antipathy
Surely there was no reason to investigate
A germaphobe in a lavatory

Russian otolaryngologists do a great job
With the auditory health of their people
The GRU heard your emphatic plea
And acceded with gleeful lethality

WikiLeaks is feeling spurned
You used to love them then demurred
Can't be easy for friends cast aside
Assange may well have been a Kurd

With incisive surgical precision
William Barr obfuscated Mueller's findings
Yet even so he does not compare
To the haze of your wily meanderings

XXVII

Pre-existings brought us great trepidation
Now this pandemic has added to our fear
We patiently await the beautiful plan you promised
Till then we must endure Obamacare

When you win by a landslide in November
Focus on healthcare like you did The Wall
You've got to lock this sucker down for real
You tried Hydroxy now it's time for Adderall

It's bewildering our Stable Genius
The Power Industry wants to comply
To Obama limits on harmful pollutants
Though you want to kiss them goodbye

No need to spell it out Stable Genius
OBAMAGATE is as clear as the tan on your face
We're not quite certain of its genesis
But there's no question something took place

We applaud the gesture Stable Genius
You've never been a phony
Let the next guy unveil Obama's portrait
It'll be a dark and classless ceremony

Birtherism to Obamagate is all of a piece
A campaign of constant grievances
It is peculiar our Stable Genius
That a Black man is your nemesis

JORDAN COUTHEN

XXVIII

You're a great illusionist our Stable Genius
A matchless manipulator of time and space
You make guilty pleas vanish in an instant
If anyone else it would be a disgrace

We know that Roger Stone agrees
There is no better BFF than you
He did the crime but won't do the time
He always knew you would come through

Lt. Colonel Vindman is history
You made it possible our Stable Genius
He chose honoring his oath over pleasing you
Serving two masters can be treacherous

We are elated our Stable Genius
You're the chief law enforcement man
An Attorney General's superfluous
Like orange lotion spread over a tan

We know Rog was derailed by bias
You named the judge and juror too
You called it Stable Genius
But no bias in the Senate towards you

We'd like to thank you Stable Genius
For saving Roger Stone
With Barr in charge at Justice
We'd say you found Your Lawyer Cohn

XXIX

Someday they'll find those emails
The server will turn up
The archaeologists will shout eureka
Finally it's a wrap

Mueller is like Greta Garbo
He wants to be left alone
That's good for you our Stable Genius
Many insist he could still be a millstone

The Pentagon Papers shed light on the truth
Nixon's recordings were crucial
What you shared in Helsinki with Putin
Must forever remain confidential

We must acknowledge we are nonplussed
You're always humble in Vlad's presence
People have been heard to say
It's a sign of some malfeasance

It's been reported Vlad paid Taliban to kill US
You said it many ways that you were never told
We fully empathize it wasn't your department
Was it consigned to Jared's portfolio

We own up to our mistakes our Stable Genius
We should have had no fear of Robert Mueller
Your stalwart confidence should have sustained us
Henceforth we will always be in your corner

XXX

Angry disgruntled Federal employees
Shouldn't testify before Congressional committees
Whistleblowers are really ratfinks
Who deserve to sleep with the fishes

It's worth a mention once again
To thank you for our strongman friends
With so many enemies here at home
We see why Vlad's the Living End

With malice towards none …
No one can live such a life
We look to your example Stable Genius
It has paid to be adept at causing strife

Disgusting despicable disgraceful
The good things you say about the Press
Your Truth and honest assessments
Gives the lie to their tedious protests

We should get our news from you only
If we want the unvarnished truth
The Press is the Opposition Party
They're the Mail-in you're the Polling Booth

Democrats Collude With Foreign Pathogen
Is what the headline should read
The Fake News won't be short of good sources
Since many Republicans also have the disease

XXXI

What's this we hear about Shithole countries
They've done better than us with the virus
Obviously the Fake News is at it again
Reporting poop spread by WHO zealots

Stable Genius it must be infuriating
Denying reports that are false and unjustified
However we are slightly confused
Why are false reports classified

If one is liberal or politically correct
Kung Flu may sound racist we guess
You do not answer to either appellation
Anyway it's the kind of thing we expect

We can't believe the fuss they made
Over the Ukraine and Russia Hoax
Though perfect call and no collusion
They misled lied and provoked

The Fourth Estate isn't Real Estate
They're even more difficult to deal with
Black female reporters get to question you
Can't get much more horrific

With Bluster and Invective locked and loaded
You make and change the rules
You get to choose your victims too
Very Stable Genius ringmaster at the zoo

XXXII

People are befuddled Stable Genius
You do everything in plain sight
You seem to have no fear of reprimand
Then again you're always right

Hannity Ingraham Dobbs
Friends not quite as genius but prime
We are ecstatic they provide wise counsel
Such selflessness is rare in these times

Your FOX News Cabinet said to open it up
The economy's been inside long enough
The doctors said it's not time as yet
Doubtlessly you will call their bluff

Covid-19 isn't Shifty Schiff
So said the WSJ
If they were the ones ruling the lectern
They too would revel in the power play

We aren't sure what Arbitrary Fascism is
But we like that your Tucker said it
We think the subtext is quite vivid
With repetition we'll make it a hit

Your celebrity is off the charts
You're bigger than the Kardashians
If you should lose two million viewers
You'd still have your base of deliriums

XXXIII

We know you took no pleasure in this
Though we must concede we did
As our VP threw shade on Jonathan Karl
We smirked like a naughty kid

We are insane about your Pressers
Viewership is through the roof
You are a god among men Stable Genius
Comparable only to the Olympian Zeus

Again female Blacks with microphones
How dare they rise to question you
Though not your type our Stable Genius
Bet you could show them a thing or two

You're a giant of media Stable Genius
There's no need to invest a dime
You're always above and below the fold
On a never-ending loop in prime time

Barr taught you about plenary authority
The fifty states are your fiefdom
The Fake News asks too many questions
It may be time to curb Press freedom

Your predictions are fantasy experts say
You're fabulist by nature and temperament
Unequipped for anything but spectacle
Spewing misinformation to malcontents

DIET
HYDROXY
CLEANSING
ELIXIR

XXXIV

You're disciplined our Stable Genius
You do not drink or smoke
We'd like you to do us a favor though
Go easy on the Diet Coke

We are enraptured in your presence
The great rallies that bind us together
We wait in breathless anticipation
Your regal emergence from the bunker

You seemed so stoic our Stable Genius
The visage of a solemn man
Whatever brought you up from the bunker
Must have been part of a holy plan

A senator said that gassing protestors
Is really in the eye of the beholder
Let it never again be said Stable Genius
Your supporters have no sense of humor

You know we are nuts about your AG Barr
He never fails to delight us
That pepper spray is not a chemical irritant
Had us in tears from uncontrollable laughter

For a man whose hands won't win awards
You've used them to great effect
Innumerable momentous flawless Tweets
Directing the Cabinet to genuflect

XXXV

We approve of your cronies and sycophants
They do what you tell them to
These are the people we want around
The perfect mixture for a can-do retinue

So deeply immersed in the job as you are
You're not like those Do-Nothing Democrats
Again and again you deliver for us
Unlike that golfing alien loser Barack

You protect us when our governors fizzle
You make so many good moves
There isn't a thing you could ever do
Which we would fail to approve

There are very bad people outside
Doing very bad incredible things
When we see these lunatics out in the streets
It's a blessing you approve of our AR-15s

New barriers around the People's House
Compel us to repeat ourselves
You ARE the master of fortifications
Our defender who quells and repels

It was a beautiful thing to see
Back when Occupy Wall Street was set free
The police swooped in to DOMINATE
Just as you did in DC

XXXVI

If looting starts then shooting starts
The scale is balanced by the ammunition
You have a lust for justice Stable Genius
Play fair when in a dominant position

Justice is incidental to law and order
FBI Director Hoover authored that gem
Now you're the LAW & ORDER President
Funny Roy Cohn and he were very close friends

Even turtles can climb fallen trees Stable Genius
Looters are easy to criticize
It's a conundrum though having once said
There are very fine people on both sides

A brick's no different than a bullet
There has got to be RETRIBUTION
People must be arrested and imprisoned
Barr will ensure due process isn't a problem

These protestors aren't your voters
The national guard should take care of them
Actually it may be a lesson well-taught
If active duty troops handle their anarchism

We know you want to keep America great
Now it's Kent State except in the streets
If we cannot count on Esper to dominate
There must be someone at Joint Chiefs

XXXVII

A reality TV approach to very serious problems
Daily episodes in which you vanquish rivals
Unique among the men who've led us
You have the advantage of all those dress rehearsals

Suburban housewives know their place
That's why they don't live in the city
Our men control them Stable Genius
Adherence to our orthodoxy keeps them pretty

It hardly need be said our Stable Genius
There's a reason you say wives instead of women
Let Democrats renounce the natural order
Our females favorite place is still the kitchen

These other women keep persisting Stable Genius
What ever happened to the old coquette
They have opinions you did not give them
We think it's obstinacy not kismet

Yoohoo what's up with our cohort
Trying to debase a female from the other side
He called her names but didn't grab her
Unlike you he seems a neophyte

Fauci's in the spotlight again
Though he remains in your doghouse
He got to throw the Nationals' first pitch
If you were the type you'd be right to grouse

XXXVIII

Slighted bitter hateful educated people
Wear mask because they don't like you
Slighted bitter hateful uneducated people
Don't wear masks because they like you

The conspicuous Tim Scott called it indefensible
He said we should take it down
We're sure he doesn't mean White power
Just a Tweet posted by some clown

We are not monolithic our Stable Genius
Some of us sometimes ask why
Does he really give a damn about us
Then we see the others and justify

Yet at times it still grates Stable Genius
You seem to anticipate our gullibility
Though we think it's the Good Book in your hand
It would be nice not to have the ambiguity

Alveda King was not a good listener
You said clearly it was A bible not yours
Hard to believe Black pastors support you
One more reason we know you were sent by God

We for one are pleased Stable Genius
The Blacks seek equality and not revenge
We concede there may be just cause for the latter
With four more years you'll make amends

XXXIX

Failed generals and admirals are jumping ship
We are comforted you know more than they
Mattis Kelly Mullen Myers Thomas Powell
Disloyal to you and therefore to the USA

We told you before we are not monolithic
We do not all set the same limits
When your Tucker says Duckworth hates America
Some of us have to say hold on a minute

Lisa Murkowski has always been shaky
Now she's hooked up with bogus Mattis
Her courage of convictions is a show of weakness
Your campaign to oust her must be ruthless

The other side has a myopic obsession with you
They can't accept your sterling stewardship
It's hard for them to see our Stable Genius
They seem to think you never had a grip

You are brave and heroic Stable Genius
It took courage to do the China ban
Many said you're racist and xenophobic
Though it had nothing to do with the Koran

They say that ignorance is symptomatic
It makes it easier to recruit
You love the uneducated as they love you
And conscious disregard for the truth

XL

About your photo op Milley now says
His part should not have occurred
He thinks he should have disobeyed your orders
Is he not on board for November 3rd

You are indefatigable Stable Genius
200 Tweets in a day
With time left to lead and govern
You still play more than a Top-40 deejay

How outstanding is Stephen Miller
He's attuned to things we condone
We're glad to know should you lose him
In the wings waits Alex Jones

Forced family separation is a thing
We'd expect a Breitbart alumnus to wage
We freely admit it was a mild surprise
You acceded to putting Brown kids in a cage

Northern Trianglers don't belong here
They worsen the American carnage
Guatemala Honduras El Salvador
Brown alien swarms with too much baggage

Subtly you changed that racial narrative
With the ingenious plan you devised
When you shut the door on those Continentals
Norwegians were also barred

XLI

Still we get how the bleach and light thing
Ties in with immigration policy
Illegals who survive the treatment
At least would be whiter internally

Chain migration is reprehensible
Time to slaughter that gorging monster
Wow Stable Genius we're so relieved
FLOTUS and parents had time for supper

A special shout out to Narendra Modi
He gave you crowds and pageantry
It's grand to meet a fellow traveler
Who wants his country Muslim-free

You are the Top our Stable Genius
Speaker Pelosi is the Nadir
So she prays for you continuously
Two Corinthians and a Holy Rosary

We wish those Do-Nothing House Democrats
Would stop sending bills to McConnell
His only job is to pack the Bench
With judges who're your adherents

National emergency two very big words
Who knew seven syllables could be so huge
Like the number of floors at your NY Tower
Probably a product of subterfuge

XLII

Covid-19 is no threat you had said
Just a cub in the path of a raging bull
No worry about our Four Oh One Kays
A bountiful spring was in store for us all

A hundred-plus-countries pandemic
Who would ever believe such a thing
We're overjoyed to have you to lead us
So much better than that guy in Beijing

You stated in your statement Stable Genius
That some states are not in the same state
However a state that is out of state
May return to the original state of that state

Deflect and blame while taking credit
Is a transcendent mode of conduction
Your style of leadership is second to none
It is beyond the grasp of anyone

Though only a quarter of China's population
We exceeded their virus numbers
With you as our leader Stable Genius
It almost feels like we are the Uighurs

A recession as you've made plain
Is far deadlier than a pandemic
Much more morbidity and mortality
And less chance for political magic

XLIII

Every time Fauci talks the market falls
He needs a zipper under his mask
Kudlow and Navarro both know healthcare
Surely like Jared they can multi-task

We embrace your heroic actions
Your constant destruction of norms
Though many shake their heads in disbelief
You will be remembered for your reforms

It's happening to you alone our Stable Genius
You shield us from the daily trauma
You shoulder all our burdens
It's clear to us you deserve the bunker

Presidents are supposed to deal with crises
Yours however never take a break
If ever you changed and said woe is me
None of us would think you a bellyache

There's method to your madness Stable Genius
You're not just any other thin-skinned despot
You know how to control the conversation
True today as in any other epoch

We're grateful to have the leader we wanted
The students were ready the leader appeared
Your elevation was doubly providential
You brought with you that journeyman Jared

XLIV

We are delighted with your senior advisor
His portfolio so wide and deep
He protects our national stockpiles
From governors who seek to deplete

We read somewhere that in normal times
Nepotism is merely corrupt
Why we mention it here our Stable Genius
Must be subliminal or a malaprop

Jared planned to send covert transmissions
Kelly counseled Kislyak to wait
Junior skulked with Russians for calumniations
You remained the immaculate candidate

Thank you once more our Stable Genius
For draining out the swamp
For Saint Mikey Pence an incredible cabinet
Those fabulous rubber stamps

You had been a wartime President
Long before Covid-19
Fighting the Press and the Congress
In types of battles not previously seen

You are the kind of man who can
Proclaim victory before victory's won
Because Stable Genius
You're that kind of man

XLV

Yes we'll fill the pews our Stable Genius
On Easter Sunday we'll rise again
We'll sing hosannas and hallelujahs
To your great American resurrection

You never fail to use your wizardry
When vacillating experts flail about
You lift the spirits of the afflicted
Your remedies are never in doubt

Praise their valor and disregard safety
That's a tactic we think is swell
These essential workers love flattery
Something Stable Genius you know so well

Too bad about Mitt's self-quarantine
Came weeks too late to matter
Considering his impeachment behavior
That seems a real nonstarter

Though Fauci's no apprentice
You managed to make him a star
The Presidential Medal of Freedom was close
But with you he got the cigar

You'd think he'd show some gratitude
His disagreeing has gone too far
We know you are the wiser Stable Genius
Your genetics are alarmingly superior

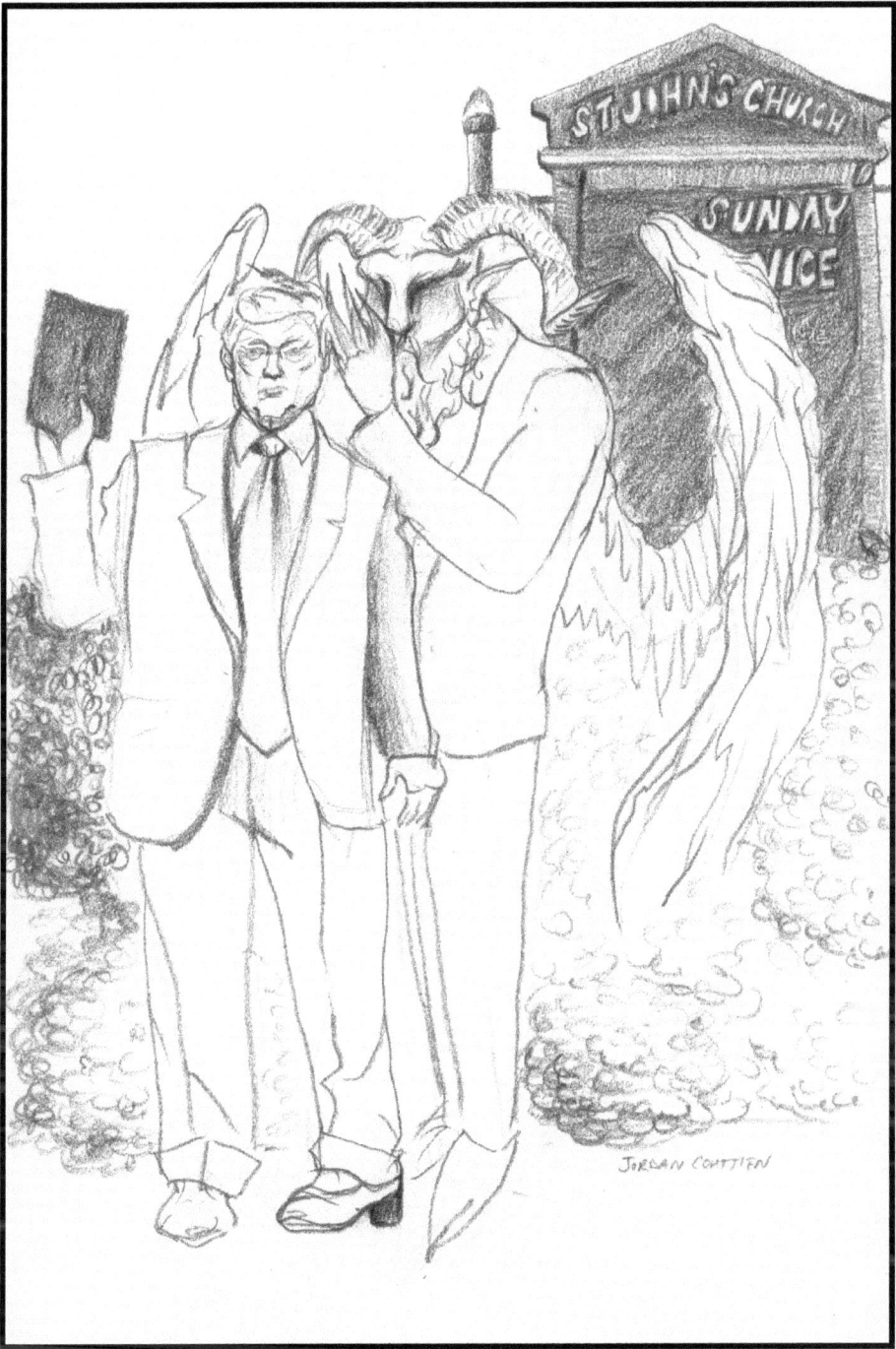

XLVI

You are prescient our Stable Genius
On May Day we'll declare victory
Guided by your gut and base
We'll have a LIBERATION rally

Head of government fights his own policies
A contradiction hiding in plain sight
Another classic Stable Genius gambit
Feign left then shuffle quickly to the right

We know we said we are partial to Nero
But there is also Jekyll and Hyde
In any persona you're still a stable genius
That's well-established and certified

As a student of history you are aware
The public can never be underestimated
Untruthful bungling ineptitude
May be your ticket to being re-elected

It's the 2nd inning not the 2nd wave
Blind physicians mixing metaphors
They should own up to their mistake
Leave the future for you to decipher

Thank you for the medical breakthrough
You alone knew it could be possible
Why should clinical trials be needed
When you've assured us it's a miracle

XLVII

We take you seriously but not literally
We will not inject bleach into our lungs
We do like the idea of a sunlit interior
UV rays to keep us forever young

Three extra months to file our taxes
We feel we have got it made
Though we must 'fess up it's not a surprise
Not sharing taxes is your stock in trade

We like that you practice social distancing
From those who do not praise you
A sure-fire way to stem the contagion
Of deference-deficient jadrools

You have such good friends Stable Genius
We like Koch Adelson Murdoch Mercer
They are true icons of social distancing
The spaces between us couldn't be wider

You do not think that healthcare
Like guns is an inalienable right
Healthy or sick is of no concern
If we are unprepared for THE fight

Let's make it clear our Stable Genius
You are The Conservation Maven
Sterilizing face masks to reuse is inspired
We like the number seventy-seven

XLVIII

It's a two-way street our Stable Genius
Your modus operandi is unchanging
There is no quid without pro quo
Governors have trouble comprehending

Your government's not a shipping clerk
You run a country not a store
When moocher states come asking for help
You are right to show them the door

We salute the attempt our Stable Genius
To trickle down the stimulus bill
Somehow the Schumers turned it around
Instead of playing the shill

One billion plus sent to dead people
Stimulus checks signed by you
They are symbolic of the Democrats lies
It proves Republican liberality in our view

We can't understand why they'd do it
Change the rules to keep you at bay
Who better to control a slush fund
You Stable Genius must demand total sway

The US is not Venezuela
Say no to the Defense Production Act
It's a Trojan Horse to Socialism
You Stable Genius could never hide in that

71

XLIX

We find no fault with this our Stable Genius
Extensive testing will find more cases
You told your people to slow it down
That should help mitigate the losses

Why do testing to make yourself look bad
Tillerson called you moron but not dumb
People should step up to stop the spread
You're not to blame when they succumb

What's up with Doctors Birx and Fauci
They aren't on the same page as you
They want to do more testing not less
Mutiny's become a habit with your crew

Like Brutus and Julius Caesar
Many on your team have been put asunder
You should have surrounded yourself with fat men
The lean and hungry seek to have you for supper

John Bolton said you're not fit to lead
He's concerned after his turn in the White House
Though we're pleased he rejected Shifty Schiff
He still turned out to be a louse

We may have already noted this affliction
A penchant for disputing your own statements
We guess it's a form of misdirection
Though it seems like a symptom of derangement

L

Anyone who wants a test can get one
We do believe you Stable Genius
But Amazon's always out of stock
Other retailers are even less propitious

You were most brilliant Stable Genius
Only sixty thousand deaths so far
Your response has been a great success
You and Jared were spectacular

Jared assures us there'll be no 2nd wave
You have no greater maestro than he
He's proven his worth to you time and again
Priceless with MBS and Jamal Khashoggi

Never made it to fifty they say
Will never make it to fifty no way
Surveys and polls are nothing to you
About as believable as the Steele Dossier

The Others question your competence and decency
Oblivious to the pre-eminence of hierarchy
What really matters is who you are
A stable genius with a winning biography

We are incredulous our Stable Genius
You're not an intellectual delinquent
You do not lack gravity and clarity
You do not prevaricate incoherently

LI

Like shotgun blasts into the face
Our Justices have turned political
Decisions not favoring conservative Republicans
Should be automatically deemed unconstitutional

We thought Gorsuch and Kavanaugh were hundred-percenters
All-in for you to the very last
We're dismayed that they've been coming up short
Looks like we may have been wrong to typecast

The O in the acronym set you off
We sympathize our Stable Genius
You've been misled of its true meaning
World Hails Obama is erroneous

Rudy Giuliani your legendary mouthpiece
He said truth isn't truth
So just as with you our Stable Genius
They will need to be reintroduced

A small man in search of a balcony
Jimmy Breslin said this about Giuliani
We heard somewhere that also could be you
Though it would be widened to hold your vanity

Of course there are reasons to despise McCain
The fake captured-hero thing is well-established
Then there was his thumb down for the ACA
Something noble he could've finally accomplished

LII

If it's Tulsa it must be Juneteenth
Jacksonville it's Ax Handle Saturday
You know how to pick 'em Stable Genius
That's why you were the envy of the Gaming Industry

It's really been annoying Stable Genius
The slanted jokes about your posture
Now that we've seen the lifts on your shoes
That should end all the unbalanced conjecture

Were you shaken by a ramp and a glass of water
We only ask because you brought it up
It's not the kind of thing you should dwell on
We'll write it off as a slip and rare misstep

When you threw that glass in Tulsa
We recalled the time Obama dropped a mic
While he was crude and graceless Stable Genius
You were refined and statesmanlike

Tulsa After-Party Walk of Shame
Yours was the look of an exhausted man
You gave it your all our Stable Genius
Your heart and soul and much of your tan

A man claiming to be a prophet said to us
When it comes to failure you never disappoint
He was living on the sidewalk in a box
Insisted that someday you'll be in the joint

LIII

A six-year old asked us Stable Genius
If policemen are killing Smurfs
Said she knows Black people matter
Who are the Blue ones getting hurt

Finally a leader who speaks up for us
For generations they've marched in the streets
Police kill us in far greater numbers
Let's stop pretending we give a shit

Who's better than you our Stable Genius
Jeff Sessions is again showing his loyalty
You kicked him and gave him no quarter
Do you want a man with so little dignity

We are extremely pleased about Roger Stone
You saved him from doing the time
He's lucky not to have toppled a Confederate statue
No way could you have commuted that crime

Because you are astute our Stable Genius
We know you must have mastered doublespeak
The fact that you've been so direct and honest
Is proof positive this is an Anti-You Pandemic

We aren't a mindless group our Stable Genius
We thoughtfully chose you to be our leader
If wearing a mask would save our lives
You would suit up faster than Lone Ranger

LIV

Students who love you are smarter than Democrats
That's why they don't wear masks
They rally undistanced during a pandemic
Certain that Fauci's a certifiable quack

If Covid-19 was a Confederate statue
States could quarantine it from the public
That would foment disorder Stable Genius
Since you'd be fighting to free it

The Confederacy lost the war Stable Genius
Those monuments you love show the opposite
It appears that history was transmuted
The Lost Cause won when we became complicit

The liar Bolton that everyone hates
Called the White House a pinball machine
That makes you the wizard Stable Genius
Playing blind but always winning

As dissenters try to unravel our democracy
It's fortuitous that you are supreme
You have correctly interpreted Article 2
Which says you don't even answer to HIM

We are in a war our Stable Genius
So you have repeatedly said
Our invisible enemy will be defeated
As soon as The Market is no longer red

LV

The world is a very angry place
You said you read about it
China and India fighting over a border
A pandemic that continues to kill

Never let a crisis go to waste
Democracy is not inevitable
We are far from the Others in terms of values
It would be just desserts for calling us deplorables

Encouraging extrajudicial killings
Is the job of the Commander in Chief
Fending off thugs burning buildings
Is a core constitutional brief

Jonathan Swan thought he had your number
You were well-prepared with charts and graphs
How could anyone not adore those drawings
We bet the kid who made them got a pass

Some Others are now calling you the First Exposer
We wondered why your past was back in vouge
We've been informed it's 'cause you've gone maskless
We much prefer the connotation of old

It just occurred to us our Stable Genius
We have never said how much you make us laugh
We hope you can forgive this lapse in judgment
We know how much you hate faux pas

LVI

We've always accepted this our Stable Genius
Your guesses are the same as unassailable facts
The few who question your veracity
Tend to also talk about adverse carbon impacts

You've read the manuals
You've read the books
Whatever they contain
Lets you off the hook

We winced as we watched you and Jonathan Swan
There were times when we nervously giggled
Where did he come up with those faces he made
Your ingenuity left him bedazzled

It's hard to believe anyone is still poor
Given the greatest economy you made before
There was enough time to save for today
Even the Blacks got their feet in the door

Crazy Nancy has gone completely insane
Treating the pandemic like a gravy train
Talk of trillions for the ninety-nine percent
Is undeniable proof why she should be in restraints

Cruel and reprehensible is a tad strong
Railing against your well-earned weekend of golf
The bad things happened the first of the month
It is what it is till the stimulus bill's resolved

LVII

Chaos and bloodshed will reign with The Other
He won't defend the American way of life
We must protect our buildings and statues
Only you Stable Genius can prevent that strife

Viruses will come and they will go
Can't allow the greatest economy to slow
It's all about the S&P and Dow
The Index and the Average are like now

Let's make it two for two
Our country will never be stronger
We agree you've gotten handsomer
And all of your things are nicer

You are complete our Stable Genius
Incumbent and Insurgent in one
Though your record may seem insurmountable
When you replace yourself you will get it done

As Armageddon is feted by The Others
Our children are ensconced in your bosom
We've taught them to use their long guns
They'll thicken the Blue Line with their martyrdom

We hear that elections are run by the states
That means you can't stop the ballots
What might we do to ensure victory
Could we go back to trying Benghazi

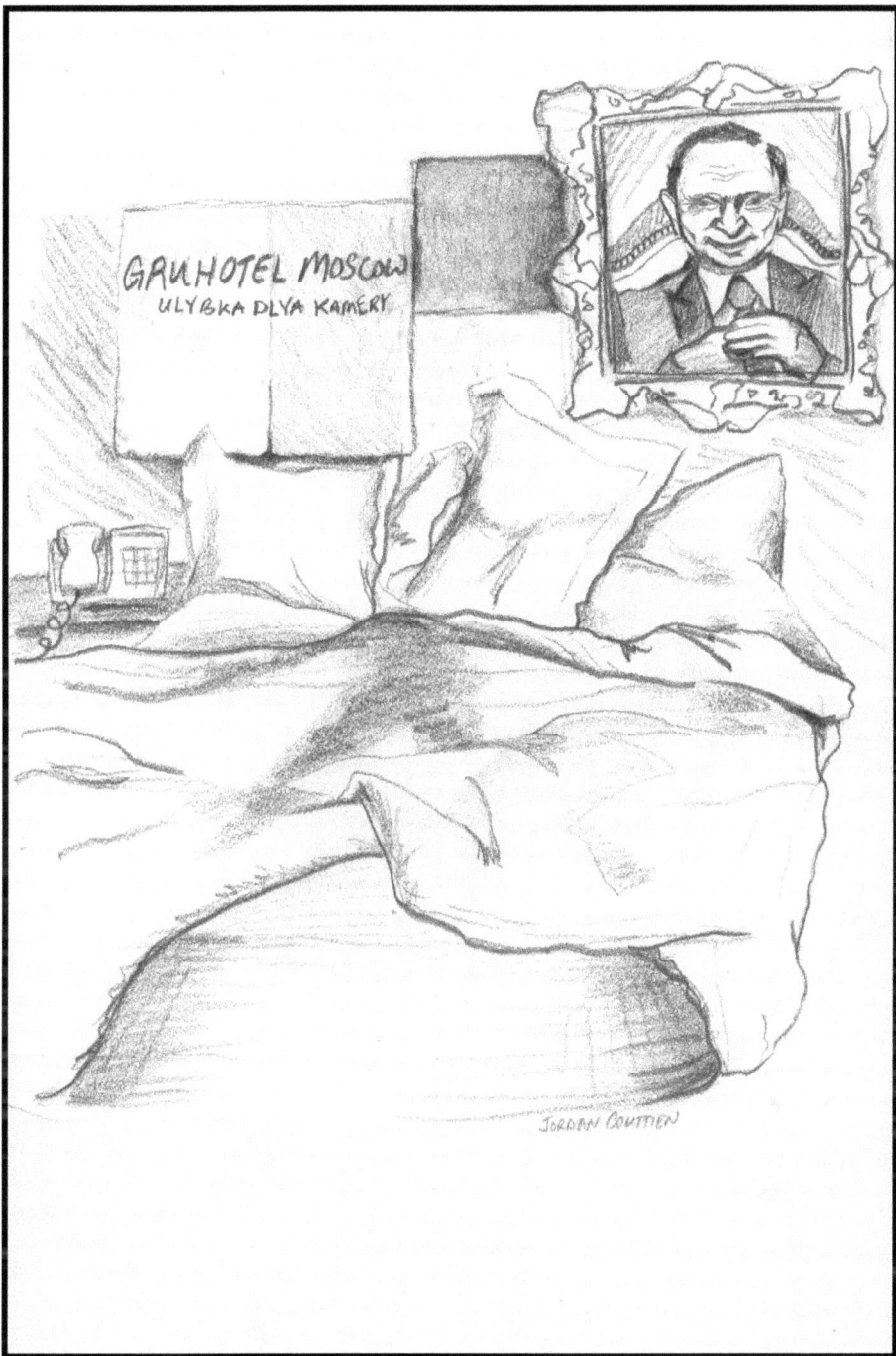

LVIII

What is Derangement Syndrome after all
Other than unconditional love
That's what most people pray for
You Stable Genius get it in droves

We just found out the census isn't rocket science
After all the years we spent in school
You never cease to amaze us Stable Genius
Counting only citizens can be done by any fool

Last night we overheard an Other say
Sounds like Stable Genius is delusional
That's akin to shouting fire in a theater
The 1st Amendment is too liberal

It's time to take them to the woodshed
Remind them you're still in charge
A little close contact discipline
Is a surefire balm for nasty-lady reportage

We see you gave up the subtlety
Brought out men who're trained to fight
We hope you first sought Vlad's advice
And not just rolled the dice

As long as Bill Barr is boss at Justice
His OLC remains a sacred cow
Extraordinary Rendition was child's play
Let anyone try and stop you now

LIX

Democrat streets are really dangerous
You must use the DHS
What's the point of a secret police
If a crime is required for an arrest

The thought never occurred to Congress
When they created DHS
That someone like you would come along
To use it against democracy's interests

They asked you not to use Reagan's likeness
Though he once called you Mr. President
Those chimps who now run his show
Must think he's the coin of the realm

She's from a shithole country Stable Genius
Female of course and Black to boot
Though the doctor's a big fan of Hydroxy
Shouldn't all that baggage make her license moot

You must have laughed your butt off Stable Genius
As Nadler's Nasties endured Barr's master class
The Thug Life must be tattooed on Bill's torso
Wouldn't be surprising given his bullying past

Mothers in Portland practicing justice
Confronting the militia you sent
Resembles an alien invasion Stable Genius
Where melanin was sucked from their pigment

LX

We cherish the truth of alternative facts
What would we really know without them
You've filled our heads with lofty matters
Instead of things brazenly ad hominem

Our wives understand biblical submission
They will fight to the death to keep it
They would not dare slap our hand away
Retribution would be swift and Catholic

A neighbor of ours who we can't figure out
Told us he was thinking how special you are
He's long been in awe of your level of genius
Now Yo Semites just moved the bar

You're clear that the pandemic of 1917
Ended World War II in 1945
Not unlike what Typhoid Mary did
To halt the Civil War in 1865

Jesus loves the little children
We know you feel the same our Stable Genius
You show great concern for their education
Your dedication to their learning is A+

Corey[sic] Booker is a scary man
Well-educated articulate and Black
A guy like him can't be allowed in suburbia
We took our women there to get away from that

LXI

Voting by mail is rigged you said
Dishonest and not transparent
If doubt about this still remains
Mitt's disapproval bolsters your argument

The polls still undercount your supporters
You'll have the last laugh once again
As Sleepy Joe snoozes in his basement
Your sleeper voters are swilling caffeine

We're more likely to be struck by lightning they said
Than for there to be voter fraud
Remember how the odds were against you winning
When the counting was done who guffawed

You have special undisclosed emergency powers
Why not postpone the election date
Though you won the one that was rigged in '16
You really ought not tempt fate

Good gambit Stable Genius
The Libs are pulling out their hair
They're fearing and despairing
A little tweet has raised big fear

We should have thought about this sooner
We're not as quick as you it's true
Since it's obvious you'd win a fair election
There's no point seeing the next one through

LXII

Out in broad daylight our Stable Genius
You've espoused your views about voting
Though out of sync with democratic principles
We applaud your boldness for not hiding

It was only a matter of time Stable Genius
Before they degraded themselves and protested
Using a subliminal word from your past
Saying you should leave the Post Office unmolested

As Chauvin pressed his knee into George Floyd's neck
Bystanders noted he seemed to be enjoying it
Many are saying you feel pleasure from their pain
By forcing their in-person ballot

Others are saying they'll risk their lives
To cast a ballot in November
We think they are mostly Democrats
Trying to incite their Republican neighbors

We find ourselves in a curious position
Our loyalty to you has been unconditional
But we're feeling uneasy about the USPS
What you're willing to do just seems unnatural

Reporter Dáte asked if you regretted lying
We were as perplexed as you
Rhetorical questions are a waste of time
Maybe now he knows it too

LXIII

We read somewhere to be pro-American
We have to be anti-You
This came with high praise for a speech by Obama
The pundits continue to misconstrue

Traitorous losers are coming out of the woodwork
Claiming you didn't grow into the job
We think you're bigger than ever Stable Genius
Your recalcitrance to redirection keeps you on top

We've noted it in several places Stable Genius
Your longstanding propensity towards autocracy
Some former believers now say it's a disqualifying trait
We are dumbfounded by their obvious hypocrisy

How silly is the Hatch Act our Stable Genius
Everyone knows you're not into boundaries
To give your Acceptance at the White House or Gettysburg
Jibes perfectly with your sensibilities

Let's make it clear our Stable Genius
This truth is nothing new
When we elected you to be our leader
We knew the rules did not apply to you

What a spectacle what a show
You're P. T. Barnum redux
We loved those well-place scripted flubs
Even more than the pyrotechnics

LXIV

There's more than one way to skin a cat
Our grandmas use to say
Mail-in fraud can't be an issue
If there's no Election Day

Mitch did a great job with the judges
While people worked and went to sleep
You'll leave a bench both deep and wide
The magnum opus of your brilliant leadership

There may be others among the hundred
But we know you cotton to Tom
Arkansas elected a staunch Republican
President to Il Duce will cause him no qualms

We know you do not drink our Stable Genius
But we would like to raise a glass to you
You're like that Latin thing a rara avis
Your true value is called into question too

We're growing concerned our Stable Genius
November may not bring a celebration
More troubling still is what may follow
As prosecutors vie for your conviction

We'd like to thank you Stable Genius
We pray you'll be given the time
A solitary place where you'll rest and ponder
Not doing so would be a crime

LXV

You fixed the broken country you were left
Where it was dark you made it bright
You're the smartest richest the very best
The enduring glow of an eternal gaslight

We'd like to thank you Stable Genius
For reminding our republic
That tyrants can't be welcomed here
If it's our intent to keep it

Though we came a long way Stable Genius
We shall not claim we were exhaustive
There's far too much to be said about you
We'll have to be content with comprehensive

This is not the apocalypse Obama said
On your glorious day of victory
Speaking of you Bill Barr would later assert
One of the greatest travesties in American history

Donald Rumsfeld used to say
We have known unknowns
Obama knew what he did not know
You Stable Genius must call Tyrone

And so we thank you Stable Genius
For what historians will say
America was a great nation
And Donald Trump made it that way

* * *

EPILOGUE

Epilogue

Speak truth to power is a standard phrase
Connected to profiles in courage
Challenges have presented at an alarming rate
We wait for someone to step up to the plate

He is the only one that matters
The only one that matters is he
He knows it and he's told it
It's all about me me me

He's told us we are lucky he's our leader
The Other will destroy democracy
They'll take away our guns and heritage
Only he can make certain we are free

So really how does one explain it
He is quite partial to autocracies
He doesn't even try to hide it
Yet legions scream in ecstasy

We've lost our love for knowledge
Long as we're entertained we're good
If we don't know Finland isn't part of Russia
It simply means we are misunderstood

Do we fight to save The Constitution
Is a more perfect union worthwhile
If there are better angels in our leader
They have never manifested in his style

This isn't Keats that would be demented
A malignant selfishness is our reality
Yet even so deep down we know
Beauty still is truth and truth is beauty

THE END

In 2016

100 million people made a difference.

They <u>did not</u> vote.

VOTE!

Vote Early.

Vote by Mail. If you can.

Otherwise …

Put on a mask.

Get to your polling place.

Wait as long as it takes.

VOTE!

www.ingramcontent.com/pod-product-compliance
Lightning Source LLC
Chambersburg PA
CBHW071353090426
42738CB00012B/3102